Did you get that!
The Art of Spiritual Shadow Work –
Volume 1

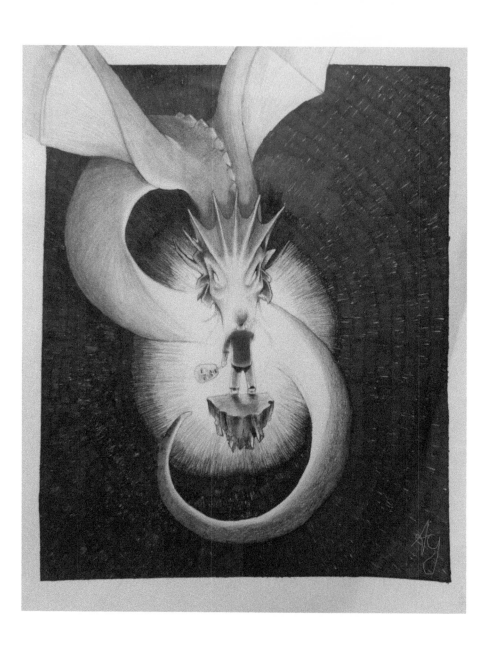

Did you get that!
The Art of Spiritual Shadow Work –
Volume 1

Bernadette Kaye

Content Editors:	Dawn and Jeff Shipley
Book Editor:	Yvette M.-C. Guy
Cover:	Amanda Jensen
Photography:	Dawn Shipley

Bernadette Kaye & Associates
2018

First Printing: February 2018

ISBN 978-1-7750534-3-9

Bernadette Kaye & Associates
202 Switzer Avenue
Ottawa, Ontario
K1Z 7H9

Email: didyougetthat@yahoo.com

Dedication

To my family and friends whose strong presence support me; to all of my Spiritual Teachers, who have made me a better person so that I may be a better guide for all of you.

To all the people helping me, I say "Thank you!" from the bottom of my heart.

Contents

Acknowledgements

The book you are about to read is the result of my wonderful students and volunteers who have helped me create the information in this work. Listed in alphabetical order: Yvette M.-C. Guy, Amanda Jensen, Dawn Shipley and Jeff Shipley. "Grateful" is not a big enough word to express my appreciation for the inspiration they have given me. Their contribution has allowed me to focus on writing the message that you are reading. They generously took care of all the details for me.

I also wish to thank all the dedicated students who have contributed to the newsletters, the set-up, translation into French and distribution over several years, one newsletter at a time. This team of workers are: Véronique Cotnoir, Sylvie Forget-Hurtubise, Sylvie Lemieux, Catherine Michaud, and Gabrielle Michaud. Perhaps one day, this book will be available in other languages. Although English is not my mother tongue, I have written all of the newsletters in the English language and the version you have now is the original one.

To you dear reader, I say open the book wherever you like. If you are reading this, your soul has been called to something higher than your day to day life. You wanted more and here it is.

With love and light,

Bernadette

Who is Bernadette?

When I first met Bernadette Kaye about ten years ago, the only question on my mind was "What is Bernadette up to?" I was deeply suspicious of her and her motives, resentful of the influence she already had over me through my wife who had, at that time, been studying under her for several years. I attended my first session with her "under duress" solely to appease my wife. When the session was over I begrudgingly admitted that what Bernadette was teaching "could be useful" but refused to commit to any further classes in the immediate future. Three years would pass before I voluntarily attended a course taught by Bernadette.

When I finally resigned to studying some of the material Bernadette was teaching I did not expect to find a healer, an alchemist, a guide, a mentor, or a friend. All I expected was to take what I could from her lessons so that I could be happier in my own life. I felt rejected by my loved ones. I believed if I could leverage what Bernadette was teaching to make them see that everything that I did that upset them was born out of a loving, selfless sacrifice for them that they would accept me again. Naively, I convinced myself that if they changed to conform to my will then the pain I felt would cease to exist. Bernadette and her teachings were the key and I needed only to take it from her. Little did I know of the path I was about to embark upon or that Bernadette was waiting to welcome me.

During my first class I learned that my problem is not "them" it is "me" and if I could "fix" myself then I could be truly happy. Regardless of my original intentions, I resolved myself to do anything to change my life and, like many of Bernadette's students before me, I asked Bernadette to teach me. In turn, Bernadette shared her knowledge so that I might learn to apply them to my own life – a life where love and fear are both necessary and healthy so that I, like her other students, might embrace my Light and my Shadow, learning the important lessons from both. The path of personal growth is not linear and it is not easy but, one by one, Bernadette nudges us all towards our untapped potential.

Almost one year after I voluntarily asked Bernadette to teach me she agreed to have me as part of her team (listed in the Dedication) to create and distribute her newsletters. As her wordsmith, it has been my honour to serve as part of the team helping to distribute her lessons as broadly as possible so that when anyone, anywhere needs them they will be there. The process of manifesting a newsletter may not always go smoothly yet that is what has made them so unique and special. Each newsletter is not just words or a topic – it reflects a point in time in the evolution of Bernadette, her team, and her students.

Seven years ago, I came to Bernadette intending to "con the con-woman" only to discover that I was conning myself. Desperate for change all I had to work with was an empty toolbox. Bernadette helped me to fill my toolbox by doing what she has done for so many people; she patiently walks with me on the path towards my own personal and unique Light.

If you were to ask me today "Who is Bernadette?" I would tell you she is a healer, an alchemist, a guide, a mentor, and a friend because she is all those things to me. Who she is to you is what you must discover for yourself. Reading the stories in this book you may begin to get a sense of what that is for you. Through these stories, Bernadette holds up a mirror lovingly pointing out what which we are too scared to believe about ourselves. She rests steadfast holding the mirror until we are able and willing to see the truth ourselves.

Then she puts down the mirror.

DO YOU GET THAT? ☺

Lots of love to all,

Jeff Shipley

Bernadette's Prayer

These messages are intended for all of you who are on the spiritual path and who are seeking concrete and practical knowledge.

I start all my workshops with a prayer I wrote long ago. I changed it a bit to adapt to this book, and its spirit remains the same. I mean every word. It is my promise to every one of you. Here it is. Make it yours if you wish.

> *I will do my absolute best to write to you with kindness, honour and compassion.*
>
> *I will do my absolute best to let go of ignorance, preconceived thoughts and limits.*
>
> *I will do my absolute best to share what may be useful to each of you without fear, anger or shame.*
>
> *I will do my absolute best to expand my understanding of other people's views and to expand my knowledge of how the world functions.*
>
> *May my words to you be honorable, true, kind and necessary.*

Introduction

Salt

"Wounds That Sting"

This anecdote is one that needs to be understood completely. It needs to be understood in one's head, heart, and bones for it is the basis of all spiritual work. It is the key to our own personal healing.

Imagine a cup of salt. There is nothing special about this salt; it could be the salt you have in your kitchen. Someone takes this cup of salt and pours it onto your bare foot. Other than there being a mess on the floor there is little else to this tale.

Now, imagine that on your foot is a long festering wound that is raw and exposed. It may be one of those wounds that we have but cannot quite remember when it first appeared. Nonetheless this is a wound that causes us great pain and discomfort.

Now, someone takes this cup of salt and pours it on this wound. The pain will be fierce and you will likely yell and maybe even cry. There is a good chance that you may curse and swear too. You will blame the salt for the pain.

Do YOU GET THAT? You will blame the salt!

What causes us pain is the wound not the salt. This wound was born in the past of this life or, in some cases, previous lives. The salt did nothing. There is nothing wrong with the salt. Salt just is. Salt does not hurt where there is no wound. It is the wound that hurts.

Many people live this life wanting their "salt" to change to "sugar" – to change the people who are the salt on their wounds. They will yell, cry, blame, swear, sulk, stonewall, get drunk, manipulate, as well as many other actions in attempt to control the pain. They do this because they are convinced that the salt is at fault. Stop blaming the salt – it is an illusion that will only make you spin. Heal the wounds with clarity, love and determination. If you chose to heal the wounds (and it is entirely your choice and within your power) salt will never hurt again...I promise.

One last thought; without the salt it is very difficult to pinpoint the location of our wounds. Salt is your friend, your ally, your teacher. It enables you to know yourself at the deepest level. Be grateful for the salt around you for it is your door to the freedom to manifest all that you truly want from your Light instead of toiling in your Shadow. Seeing the salt as your friend will prevent the victim energy from suffocating your capacity to love, create and be fully alive.

May you all welcome salt into your lives.

PONDER THIS: Who are the people who are the salt to your wounds? Can you find gratitude for them and for the self-knowledge they bring to you?

Section I: Fire

FIRE … THE WORLD OF PASSION,

THE FIRST SPARK OF LIFE AND SPIRIT.

Shadow

The concept of "Shadow" is not particularly easy to explain. Inside us all, there is a part of ourselves that we hate and hide. That hidden and hated part is what is called here "the Shadow". Unless we do the alchemical work on the Self, we do not know that we don't know. We hide the Shadow from ourselves so that we are not consciously aware of our disapproval. Without dedicated spiritual investigation, it is unlikely we are aware of the havoc our Shadows create in our day-to-day lives.

Our Shadow is responsible for the drama, the triggers, and the fights that result in the problems within our lives. Our Shadow is a powerful agent of destruction able to create its own reality and sucking us in without us ever being aware that we are being manipulated. Projection, judgement, anger, stonewalling, victimization and despair are only a few of the dark manifestations perpetuated by our Shadow. It seeks to keep us scared with confusion, isolating us from the world around us. Our Shadow prevents us from knowing our Light.

Love Answered

"Love or Fear – Your Choice"

Once upon a time, in the middle of a long night, Fear knocked on the door. Love decided to answer. When Love got to the door, there was no one there.

There are only two main emotions: Love and Fear. They are mutually exclusive. One excludes the other. The more love you have, the less fear will grip your heart. The more fear you have, the less love can heal you and those around you.

Emotions either fall under the heading of Fear or Love. It is really quite simple: it's one or the other.

Fear manifests in many different destructive energies. To name but a few, Fear is: anger, jealousy, envy, self-pity, pride, shame, greed, depression, cowardice, judgement, longing, perfectionism, boredom, and so on. Seize hold of any of these emotions and take a closer look. Scratch the surface and you will invariably find that these energies were weaved with the fiber of Fear. The foundation of these emotions is indeed Fear.

Love manifests in many different constructive energies. To name but a few, Love is: compassion, generosity, respect, gratitude, forgiveness, serenity, joy, understanding, courage, happiness, and so on. Seize hold of any of these emotions and take a closer look. Scratch the surface and you will invariably find that these energies were weaved with the fiber of Love. The foundation of these emotions is indeed Love.

To Love or to Fear is your choice. **DO YOU GET THAT?**

Many times I have been told by my students that they refuse to love because they have been hurt or humiliated in the past. Now what? Will they live their life in the past? Should they live with fear built on the past, their past will become their future. Should you make that choice, your present life will be full of fear and loneliness. What you thought was resolved is only buried alive and affects your present. Buried feelings only make you relive the past again and again to prove your Shadow right. The Shadow absolutely wants to be right. Yet your heart does not care about being right, it only wants healing.

On occasion my students have told me that they have decided to close their heart once and for all. That they are not good at relationships, that they always end up on the losing side, and that they always get the short end of the stick. Fear breeds in such thoughts. Remember that fear is only there to show you the way to growth. You need courage to face your fears. Where is your courage?

From time to time my students have told me that they are not afraid of anything; not even death! When I ask them how things are with their loved ones, they shut down. Again, this is fear. Denying fear will lead to despair, depression and loneliness. I have never met anyone who was not, on some level, afraid of fear and afraid of love.

Your Shadow recoils from the energy of love. No greater threat to your inner demons exists than letting love enter your heart! Your Shadow is fear-based and love consumes fear. Remember that there are only two main emotions: Love and Fear. If love conquers the demons constructed by your Shadow what will happen? Your Shadow will die ... your essence, your brilliance will live!

But your Shadow so wants to live! It whispers to you that your brother, lover, mother, sister or friend are out to get you. The Shadow feeds on fear, and all its iterations. It lies to you to manipulate you into feeling fear (anger, shut down, avoidance, sulking, blame, guilt, etc.) and feeds on it. Your Shadow, now stronger, continues to fuel the fire.

Love, and all the energies related to love, will release you from the infernal cycle. To love is to jump into the unknown, to risk it all and still decide to remain open. To love is to understand that pain is the only door that leads to growth. To love is to say "Yes!" to life.

To Love is to be fearless. To Fear is to be loveless.

Dare to say "*No*" to the demons of fear and "*Yes*" to all the Love around you.

One last secret dear friend: What is not love is an illusion.

May the Love in your heart open the door to Fear and, when your heart is ready to receive, you will see there is always someone waiting on the other side. They are waiting to love you.

PONDER THIS: Today, take one of your negative behaviours in one particular instance. Are you stonewalling your significant other? Are you nagging at your child? Are you angry at your colleague? Are you certain to be the victim in this event? Now find the fear inside of you. Behind the stonewalling, the nagging, the anger, the victim, is fear ... what are you afraid of? What would happen if you let go of that fear ... for one hour? For a lifetime?

Blame

"Gateway to the Triangle of Hell"

Let go of blame. Blame is the fastest and surest way to give away your power. When you choose to be in "blame mode" you have assumed the role of the victim. You are wholly convinced that you are the victim of a perceived "bully". The bully could be your lover, your sister, your parents, your boss, the government, a racial group, a social group, so forth and so on. When you blame another person or thing you give your "bully" power over you and further entrench yourself in the role of the victim.

How about expanding your reality and understanding (deeply, not just on the surface) that there are many sides to any story; that your story is only "your story"?

When you blame you have decided to be the victim. The same applies when you blame yourself. As long as you embrace your perceived victimization you will need a rescuer to move forward. What will serve to rescue you? It could be alcohol, drugs, anger, sulking, a friend, bitching, a spouse or your work.

Blame is the most effective way to ruin any relationship. Angry and depressed, you will be stuck, unable to manifest the things that you truly want.

Blame is a choice. Choose instead to create from what you learn. Be grateful for all you have, the good and the bad, and create from it what you will.

To have to blame is victim energy. To let go of blame is to become a creator. **DO YOU GET THAT?**

Watch your thoughts and be mindful that you are in charge of them. Cease to blame and reclaim your power!

PONDER THIS: Can you spend a whole day without blaming yourself or another? Instead of blame create another vision. Can you spend two days without blame?

Triggers

"The Necessity of Triggers"

To be alone can be difficult for some people while for others, it can be an escape. To be alone to escape means to make a choice based on Fear. Fear is only ever valid when faced with a life-or-death scenario like being chased by a tiger.

The more fear you have the less love you will have. We need to stop contributing to the growing deficit of love in the world.

Many times students have told me that living alone has allowed them to be more serene and calm. Their rational was simple; as long as they were alone, no one could upset them and they would feel safe. Do you feel the undercurrent of fear in their decision? Their isolation was fostered by fear; a fear of their own internal demons and an unwillingness to reconcile with those demons.

Other times students have informed me that they were spiritually advanced because they had studied many books and meditated in domestic and foreign ashrams, temples or silent retreats. Their demons remain hidden behind the pages of their books or in the mortar of the temple walls waiting to manifest themselves at a moment's notice. That moment may come at an inopportune time in reaction to a "distasteful" (distaste is relative to one's perspective) remark from a parent, boss, lover, friend and so on. Books and temples may calm your mind but they will never stir your heart.

We tell ourselves all sorts of fictions about relationships. We say we are not good at relationships; that we always end up being hurt; that we are not the dating or marrying type, and that friends always end up stabbing us in the back. We talk of siblings or parents who are never on our side. We create our reality based on these perceptions and this makes our stories seem real. This is our inner Critic talking.

Remember that we do not see people as they are; we see people as we are, since we project ourselves onto others.

Only in a relationship and in the real world can we come to know ourselves, our demons, our Shadow and our Light. **DO YOU GET THAT?**

The demons you see in others are in fact the projection of your demons!

The closer the relationship, the more opportunity to be triggered you will have. These triggers will flush out your demons and provide you with extraordinary self-knowledge and opportunities for growth and healing. You will then find serenity in your relationships. This serenity will be based on love, acceptance, compassion and generosity; not fear.

One of my teachers told me once that he took great pleasure in sending the "book and temple" people to spend a whole week with their family. Afterwards, he would receive many reports from them about how angry, frustrated, sad, rejected, and so on they had felt. If you want to get rid of the fear, and once and for all start building serene relationships based on love, you have to become aware of your inner world, and your inner demons.

Stop sowing the seeds of depression and misery. Stop fearing abandonment. Stop wanting to be right. Stop blaming others. Know that being triggered is only a tool to help you flush out your demons. It is key that you stop taking everything personally. When you are triggered, turn your focus inside and see what is going on. Be present in the moment; be with yourself. Guidance will come from within. Do not fight it. Try not to resist what goes on inside but stand apart so that you are able to look at it, feel it, observe it and then decide what the highest choice is. Stop reacting, start acting. Only then will you be able to see the truth of your own past experiences and not the truth of the story as your Critic has told it to you.

In all aspects of your life have one eye in and one eye out.

Being spiritually present in a relationship means you understand that the other person is simply a mirror of yourself. Others are not responsible for satisfying your needs. They are not responsible for your happiness. When you burden them with these responsibilities it will invariably lead to disappointment, anger, sadness, and so on. In spiritual relationships, lovers need to be gentle and kind mirrors who will give up wanting to be right and wanting to blame so that they may strive for self-actualization, love and compassion of Self, and anyone else on the planet.

PONDER THIS: What are you afraid of? Being alone? Being in an intimate relationship? Being successful? Being a failure? Whatever you are afraid of, find out how many decisions are made from this fear. What would your life look like if you made decisions from a peaceful Core?

Negativity

"Fuel of the Darkness"

Many of you have talked to me about the negative people with whom you share your life. Negativity comes in many forms: bitching, whining, complaining, belittling others, focusing on fault, sarcasm, bitter jokes – all the reflections in the proverbial glass being "half empty".

Negativity hurts and it hurts everyone touched by it. Negative words, negative body language, negative tone of voice...all of it hurts. The negative person is hurting and wants others to join them in their descent to Hell. It is contagious and it can kill friendships, destroy romances, and wound families.

When you are with a sibling, friend, partner, or colleague; why focus on their negative traits? Dwelling on the negative will only push people away from you! The "push away" is persuasive and effective. Negativity causes distances. Intimacy cannot be fostered in a negative environment.

Intimacy can only bloom when fed with love. When you are feeling negative ask yourself why you are afraid to be close to those around you?

Neediness and fragility are the product of a wounded heart and pushing people away is a means of feeling "safe". It never works. You will never find peace in fear. You will never find peace in anger. You will never find peace in sadness. You will just create more of that which nurtured your fear, anger, and sadness and end up pushing more people away.

All that will be left of this mess is a terrible, terrible loneliness. **DO YOU GET THAT!**

Negativity is based on fear. Fear of intimacy, fear of connection, and fear of being vulnerable – these are powerful drivers that require immense courage to negate: the courage to look at ourselves honestly, the courage to delicately heal our hearts, the courage to go to any length to change. I cannot do it for you. No one outside you can.

One more thing: the pain of your past – no matter how bad – can never justify negativity. Using the pain of yesterday to destroy those around you will only ensure a repeat of yesterday. To live in the past is to make the past into the future.

Darkness will beget darkness. By focusing on the darkness you will only attract more darkness. Try instead to find gratitude in all that you meet; yes, even for what you label bad or painful. In time, with courage and will, your heart will open and you will embrace your own Light. See the Light in others and shine your Light onto them. My prayer for all humankind is to find such courage!

May your heart have the courage to see the Light; both yours and that of those around you.

With Light and love (I mean that!)

PONDER THIS: For one day, refrain from using sarcasm and cynicism. For one hour, refrain from any negative thought about the world out there. For one minute,

can you have loving tender thoughts about yourself?

Doubt

"Paralysis Through Fear"

When our demons invade our energy field we begin to "doubt". Doubt causes us to lose our confidence, fearing that we will make a mistake (whatever a mistake means to you). We fear that our ego will get hurt. We lose trust in the universe.

When we doubt we are unable to commit to anything. When we doubt, we question our intelligence and will not commit to learning. When we doubt, we question our strength and will not commit to physical activity. When we doubt, we question our ability to love and be loved and will not commit to romantic relationships. When we doubt, we question ourselves and will not commit to leadership.

What is doubt? Simply put; doubt is fear.

So what are you afraid of? Most probably you are afraid of being rejected and abandoned (two of the most painful states for human beings). That fear will prevent you from fully living your life.

I have a secret for you. Doubt is not real. Doubt is fear.

Doubt always represents a lack of knowing that the Universe takes care of you at all times. **DO YOU GET THAT?**

Doubt drives us deeper inside ourselves to the murky realm of the Shadow. This realm is one where pain, self-righteousness, blame and fear rule. In this place we are prevented from being in the Now, from being our true Nature, and from love.

Doubt is the harbinger of disease, chaos, fear, poverty and all other manifestations of scarcity and pain.

Doubt is a fiction of the mind. Ah, how the mind loves to create! While the mind might seed doubt, the heart always knows the truth. So too does the body as does the spirit. Heart, body and spirit understand that doubt is a fabrication, an illusion of the mind. Yet many people will devote an entire life to these fabrications of the mind. They will make decisions using the one tool that creates doubt; the mind. The mind knows only knowledge but not wisdom. The mind cannot grasp Knowing.

Should it not make perfect sense then to follow that which does not doubt and always Knows? Should we not surrender to the wisdom of our hearts, our bodies and our spirits?

Once we are intimately acquainted with our inner knowledge of our higher self, the mind will quiet down and the aligned decisions will always be taken from a place of wisdom instead of a place of information.

Remember that the Universe loves you and takes care of you. We know this when we are born but then we forget. We presume to know what perfection is. We presume to understand divine justice. May we all have a Zen mind, free of the arrogance of the Shadow. Acknowledge the doubt, observe the fear but do not follow it...and then just move forward.

Remember that you are always loved.

PONDER THIS: When you doubt, you do not doubt about yourself but about the unfolding of the universe. When you doubt, your Shadow tells you to manipulate, control, criticize, use force, to shut out the world. Doubt is you not trusting the present moment. Make the list of what you do not trust about the universe. Give it a day or two and then destroy the list and be free.

Poison Arrows

"Projecting Pain/Anger on to Others"

When we "loose it" on someone else we actually lose a part of ourselves. Energetically, we deteriorate our own base and lower the level we are vibrating at. Sending demeaning words towards another person or situation is like slinging poison arrows across the space and into our target. When we get upset at someone we lose part of our energetic field and, some would say, we lose part of our soul.

Gossiping, insulting, negative comments and belittling are a few of the poison arrows we have in our quiver that can be exploited to hurt everyone. Stonewalling, the "silent treatment", and the calculating coldness of revenge are also arrows available in our arsenal.

Know that every thought, every intention that you have will have an impact on the people around you, an impact on yourself and an impact on the world. **Do YOU GET THAT?**

Naturally, whatever you put out there is your own issue, a projection of your Shadow, and has often very little to do with what has triggered you. The one with whom you are upset with is merely a trigger; what triggered you is your salt to your wound. It is you and you alone who carry the wound from whence spawned the arrow. The person or situation is just a mirror within which your pain is reflected back to you. This is true for all situations whether it be the parent who is angry at the child or the lover who has disdain for his or her mate.

No one has the power to make you angry, sad, guilty, et cetera, unless you have that trigger inside you already. No one can spark these emotions if you do not have a wound that will sting when plied with salt.

The next time you want to "lose it", how about you look inside yourself to find the answer? Ask yourself what your wound is and ask how you might heal it before you sling the poison arrow.

One last thought; anger, fear or shame will often appear safer than love. Anger, fear and shame lets you draw the walls close around yourself and protect your wounds in a false sense of security that numbs the pain you feel. Love asks you to open your heart and ask for others to love you unconditionally but, in the process, heals the wounds rather than numbing them.

So, my dear path companions, open your heart, love, risk exposure, plunge forward and love some more!

PONDER THIS: Next time you feel compelled to shoot a poison arrow at someone, decide that you will not be the slave to your anger, fear or shame. Instead, aim and shoot at the monster within.

Betrayal

"Control Through Betrayal & Denial of Pain"

The subject of betrayal is one that I frequently discuss with my students. What is "betrayal"? The answer often varies. Your answer probably has something to do with someone doing something mean/ cruel or unfair to you.

Spiritually, betrayal is this: someone does something to you and you get to see a part of yourself that you would rather not see. What about yourself would you rather not see? You see that you are insecure. You see that you are lonely. You see that you are undesirable, needy, afraid, stupid, and so on and so on. Betrayal is only the Mirror of what you have buried deep inside yourself and yet it is an opportunity to see what you already know. You hate the reflection in the Mirror and so you demand – or beg - that the person you are projecting yourself unto, stops behaving that way.

In an effort to shatter the image in the Mirror you may say things like:

- "Please, do not lie."

- "Please, do not sleep with another.", or

- "Please do not do this because I do not want to see what I become when you do this. I want to remain blind to what I become; I do not want to see what lurks in my own darkness."

What you are really saying is that:

- I don't want to see my own darkness.

- I want to be blind to my own shortcomings, and/or

- "Please behave the way I tell you to behave." So that I do not see me.

Betrayal is an attempt to control the image in the Mirror. We use betrayal to control the other person's behaviour reflected in the Mirror in an attempt to avoid facing our dark side, our Shadow. **DO YOU GET THAT?**

Betrayal is a door behind which is freedom from your Shadow. Insulting or hating the Mirror (the one who "betrayed" you) will only drive you to seek escape; escape through anger, victim energy, revenge, alcohol, drugs, etc.

Only when you know yourself and love yourself will betrayal cease to exist. Then and only then will you be free.

PONDER THIS: Think of one time when you were betrayed. What part of yourself did the betrayal reveal? Can you welcome and heal this part of you?

Revenge

"Projected Grief"

Picture yourself in a movie theater or at home, comfy on the couch, with a movie playing. The movie is a Western. You hear the harmonica playing and see a little house at the base of a valley. A family lives there. The father is out chopping wood with the eldest son lending a hand while the mother and daughter are focused on getting their pristine white laundry sorted out on the clothes line. A second, younger son takes the split wood, and arranges it into a neat pile behind the house. The youngest in the family (another boy) plays with the family dog. The scene is the perfect picture of an idyllic family existence on the Frontier.

Suddenly, the music darkens and a murderous gang gallops into view. The hooves of their black horses thunder as they storm towards the little house and unsuspecting family. The gang savagely kills the entire family with one lone exception; the youngest boy. The young lad manages to hide out of sight until the men are all gone. With the rampage over and the gang fading into the distance the little boy comes out from his hiding place only to see that all that he loved and held dear is gone.

The caption "Twenty Years Later..." flashes across the screen as the scene changes.

The little boy is now a man consumed with rage and thirst for "justice". He has decided the time has come to kill all the bad men who murdered his family. From the day of the murders until now the little boy has tirelessly prepared to avenge his slain loved ones. He is now one of the most feared, most accurate gunmen in the Wild West. He has a thirst for blood and is looking to quench it.

This is revenge!

He encounters the first gang member in a saloon. "Remember me?, he growls allowing only the briefest moment of recollection before he fires a single bullet with deadly accuracy straight through the man's heart. This is only foreshadowing for what will come. The little boy, now grown, tracks the second gang member to a whore house, while a third he hunts down on a ranch and so on and so on until he confronts the last surviving member of the gang. For his final act of vengeance, the little boy confronts this man at high noon in the middle of Main Street. The gang member never stood a chance and the avenger stands over his corpse awash with the knowledge that he has vanquished everyone responsible for the deaths of his family members. The good man has won. He has fulfilled his revenge!

Now what?

What was it all for? To feel better? No, not really. Staring down at the lifeless body before him he does not feel lighter, happier, or released of his anger or sadness. Did it bring his family back? Of course not. If he feels no better for all of this then why did he want to exact revenge?

He wonders to himself what is "revenge" and what exactly did he hope it would accomplish?

First, revenge is a way of alleviating grief; revenge cannot relieve grief. To live with grief and grow through it we need to embrace our pain, our sadness so that we can learn to accept the life event that caused us to feel grief in the first place. Sometimes, when our grief is too great, we seek out revenge as a means of distracting us from our grief. We seek out revenge and use it to project the pain felt in our grief onto others so that we can make them responsible for our feelings rather than taking that responsibility into ourselves. Revenge, like any distraction, can never replace the real thing.

Second, revenge is an attempt to transform shame into pride. **DO YOU GET THAT?**

The little boy was shamed by his sense of powerlessness coming from watching the murder of his family while he hid. This shame drove his quest and that shame, unaddressed, will never go away. Instead, the man's healing will only come from the compassion and understanding that he extends to the little boy still consumed with shame deep in his soul.

The man needs to embrace the truth; that there was nothing the little boy could have done to stop the murder of his family. Killing the men responsible for the death of his family will not reconcile the conflict inside him; it is only a distraction from his shame. Until the man lets go of the little boy's shame he cannot grieve nor heal.

Next time you are consumed with thoughts of revenge, arrest the imaginations and scenarios in which you exact your revenge. Instead, take a step back and ask yourself why you are avoiding your grief and of what exactly are you ashamed? If you can find the compassion to heal your shame you will find your way to peace within.

This is the true way to grieve.

PONDER THIS: Can you get in touch with your thoughts of revenge, past and present? Can you find the shame of your actions and then have enough compassion to love yourself?

Boredom

"Disengagement as Boredom – Engage in the Present!"

Often I am confronted with sighs and complaints related to a general weariness towards life. A vague anger suspended by bent shoulders and empty eyes precedes an all too familiar declaration of boredom. "My life is boring, Bernadette.", "My husband is boring.", "My job is boring.", or "My parents are soooo boooring." are frequently accompanied with a teenage-like rolling of the eyes and resigned sigh is how it goes.

Most of my students don't know what exactly bores them or what boredom really means to them. Often, they'll give me examples of things they find "boring" or they will vaguely describe their feelings, punctuated with comments like "I just don't like it." Truly, this has no meaning.

Functionally, they all will agree their boredom is uncomfortable, even painful, but rarely are they able to pinpoint the source of their boredom. Resigned to their inability to define the source of their struggle, they retreat into analogies telling me a story about how boring their job, a person, et cetera is in order to convince me. If you could define "boredom" what would it look like?

Boredom is an unwillingness to engage. DO YOU GET THAT?

Nothing exists on this planet that is inherently boring. Our perception jades our opinion on what is and is not boring. No person, no job, no task, no family member, no life is boring unless you refuse to engage with it!

Through engagement, we connect with that which exists outside ourselves. Whether we connect or not is entirely up to us. The more we know ourselves the more we can respect, honour, and love ourselves. Through our intimate acquaintance with Self we can connect with the world and people around us with love and acceptance.

When confronted with a difficult connection, like those times we are "bored", we are confronting a part of ourselves that we do not honour. Nothing less and nothing more.

"Out, beyond idea of right doing and wrong doing,
there is a field; I will meet you there."
- Rumi -

We must strive to nurture these sacred connections. Roaming the field is required in order to vanquish boredom from our lives. If we can do that then we will truly inhabit the present. The NOW (as it is popular to say) is the most fascinating moment of our lives because it is the only moment that exists and because it is the mirror of our Selves. The past is an idyllic or morbid painting of what we want to preserve of our experiences. The future is a chaotic abstract bursting with our hopes, fears and dreams. The present is a multidimensional sculpture that exists for a singular moment but, during its lifetime, we are afforded infinity to examine and explore the depths of its meaning. The past, the future and all the "Ifs" associated with them are escapes that reinforce our disengagement from the present. When we are disengaged boredom will surely follow.

There are many reasons why our minds will try to bolster disengagement with the NOW. These reasons are as distracting as the stories meant to illustrate the discomfort of boredom. The truth behind the justifications is simple – it is fear; fear of intimacy, fear of failure, fear of rejection, fear of hurt, fear of being seen for who we are, fear of fear. The fears are legion yet they do not need to rule our lives.

Where boredom exists our hearts are closed. When we walk with closed hearts, we can lose the present to negativity, sarcasm, cynicism, and other poisons of the soul. It is in this state that darkness can take root until we are possessed by boredom in every facet of our lives. We need to open our hearts and be willing to engage in the miracle of the present. We need to be willing to embrace the present and be open to all its possibilities and be ready to delve into the cloak of mystery that shrouds it. This, and only this, will serve to lift the darkness and banish boredom forever. Assert your influence over boredom, refuse to let it stain your joy, and choose to be free!

Engage in the moment no matter what the moment brings!

PONDER THIS: Find something you label as boring and do that thing. With all your focus, will and intent engage in it by being curious about it, by examining what is going on in your emotional body (anger, sarcasm, anxiety, victim, it's not fair) and see how much self-knowledge there is in being engaged in the now.

Change

"Stagnation to Hold on to Blame"

There is but one universal constant; change. Everything in the universe changes both in substance and levels. Nothing remains the same. Refusing change and fighting the growth that comes from, it is futile.

This holds true of relationships as well. Everyone around you is constantly changing and adapting to new energies. The metamorphosis that envelopes us all fuels change within our relationships. A day will come when someone you care about (child, spouse, lover, or friend) will tell you that things are not working and that change is needed. Or it may be you who will approach someone you care about (friend, employee, or significant other) and tell them that things are not working and that change is needed. When that day comes, the choice confronting you both is to grow or to stagnate. Should you refuse change and its opportunities for growth then the relationship will be condemned to death.

We cling to stagnation and fight change because we want to continue blaming others for our pain. **DID YOU GET THAT!**

Choosing growth is about opening our hearts wide to discover the key to the next level of our personal development. Yet we often choose stagnation because we see change as the horrible chore of admitting to being wrong, of giving something up, or of "giving in" to another. There is no one attacking you out there. The demons are within you. There is no chaos out there, only divine order. The opportunity for growth is embraced with great joy, not fear.

May the future open many doors to all of you and may you find the courage to say "Yes" to change.

PONDER THIS: Where your pain lies, is where the need to change resides. What is it in you causing you pain? How can you change? Why do you resist growth and choose pain?

Separation

"Abandoning Duality"

I know that from time to time the world may appear as though it is a forsaken place where "dog eats dog" is the rule of the day. It is a place where trusting the universe does not come easily because you have been hurt, disappointed, betrayed and the like. The key is to remember that, despite what the Shadow perceives, we are all One here in this Universe. What does this mean? Consider this: There are only atoms and space in between here and nothing else. You are made of atoms, your boss is made of atoms, and your neighbour's dog is made of atoms, as is your best friend and the ocean. These atoms are all cut from the same atomic cloth; they are all one in the same. What you are made of is the same material that your ex is made of. Despite this unalienable truth we may find ourselves feeling like we are better than the next person. Think again.

God, or whatever form your higher power assumes, makes all His creations of the same atoms.

Everything has a function and purpose. The Universe does not make mistakes. The Universe is harmony and only creates perfection (including your ex). The next time you participate in a meeting or are walking in the streets, remind yourself that everyone present is your brother and sister, that you are cut from the same cloth, you are all perfect in your own way, and they are all the same as you. You are them and they are you.

Duality fosters the agonizing "me against the world" paradigm. The illusion of duality will leave you lonely and stuck. Oneness (the understanding that we are all one) roots the "me with you" seed that will bloom while you travel the journey of life. Together as one the only real enemy you will ever encounter is your own Shadow.

We project our Shadows on to other people. We then mistake these projections of Self as our enemies. The end result is agony, anger, suffering, depression and separation. DO YOU GET THAT?

Forthwith banish the word "against" from your soul.

Spiritually, there exists no "against". Embrace

Oneness with all those around you.

May your heart heal the separation created by your

mind.

PONDER THIS: For one day, tell yourself that you are

made of the same stuff as your colleagues, your dog,

the store clerk, the politician you did not vote for, the

trees, the jail inmates. See yourself fight to remain

separate and distinct. Know that separation is a

source of pain and an illusion. Can you do this every

day?

Beauty

"Judgement Through Beauty and Ugliness"

Do you know that everything is beautiful?   When one cannot see the beauty in everything it is an indication that there is something wrong with all our senses; our ears, our noses, and, especially, our eyes.

Many of us are quick to judge something as beautiful or as ugly. When it comes to ourselves this judgement can be particularly swift and cutting – especially when we perceive "ugliness".

The truth is that there is only the ugliness that we project from deep inside upon the world around us. We trust our eyes to tell us the "truth" but they cannot see the truth. They only perceive things the way we want them to see things and not how things really are.

We see what is behind our eyes, not what is in front of our eyes. Ugliness is a projection of our Shadow. **Do YOU GET THAT?**

What is beauty to you? Is beauty perfection? Is it balance? Maybe it is peace? Efficiency? Knowledge? What? Do you know?

What is ugliness to you? Is it imperfection? Is it disharmony? Maybe it is war? Inefficiency? Ignorance? What? Do you know?

Your "ugly" is a reflection of what you do not like about yourself. It speaks volumes about you and little about the world around you.

God (Reader: please insert spiritually acceptance noun here) does not create ugliness; God only births perfection. If you cannot see this then it is your eyes, not reality, that require correction.

Come closer and I will promise you something. When you reach a state of grace, of limitless love, the whole world will exude a beauty that will take your breath away.

Once a student told me that she lived in this higher state of spiritual understanding. From this perspective she elaborated that a dead rat on top of a pile of manure could make her heart sing. She could see and feel beauty everywhere! One look at her face, basking in her smile, you knew that she was not crazy, just in a higher state of grace. She was not on drugs. She was not blissfully ignorant or a simpleton. She just "gets" beauty!

Imagine being surrounded with that type of beauty at all times and being able to reach out and taste, touch and smell a world drenched in unconditional love. All you need do is train your eyes to see without judgement or projection. Stop trying to make the world conform to your narrowly defined understanding of beauty and start opening up yourself to loving all the beauty the world has to offer.

In Kabbalah, beauty is found in Tiphareth at the center of the Tree of Life. As in any structure, when the center is unbalanced, the whole structures topples. May beauty find your Tiphareth and become the center of your life.

Oh, by the way, I find you all beautiful. I mean that.

PONDER THIS: Can you look at your reflection in the mirror and hear the voices inside your head telling you what is wrong with your body? Why do you believe those voices?

Pushing Love Away

"Learning to Let Others Love Us"

To love oneself will make you whole but to allow another to love you will make you More. Only through the love of others can the full measure of who we are be achieved. Their love reflects our Light unto ourselves and reveals the true beauty we contain within ourselves. It is only with this Light that the negative opinions we harbour about ourselves can be laid bare and melt away.

But you need to allow others to love you. Love is all around. Just let it in. Simple.

Past hurts often make us fear love. We live in the past and try to protect ourselves by thwarting love in the present. It is easy to live in the past as it is the darkness that we know; it requires courage to move forward towards our Light. When patterns of the past take hold, we quickly find ourselves without love in our lives. The absence of love creates a vacuum within us that must be filled with something else. Television, alcohol, drugs, shopping or another distraction will be used to escape the pain. None of these activities offer a permanent solution and we quickly find ourselves stuck in an endless cycle all because we lack love. Pain.

Pushing love away is easy. Being negative, critical, angry, envious, controlling, narcissistic are just some of the ways to push others away. Criticality of another is just a reflection of our own Shadow. When we label others as lazy, needy, angry, cold, and so forth we are projecting our Shadow unto the other. The label belongs to us. Love cannot grow and blossom in our Shadow.

Unconditionally loving those who cross your path will attract love to yourself because then, and only then, will you love yourself. And that will indeed make you More. We are all One and what we do not love in another is something we don't love in ourselves. As long as you reject what you don't love in yourself you invite emptiness, depression and darkness to fill the void where love is absent.

Being loved by others is a reflection of how you love yourself. **DO YOU GET THAT?**

Slay the fear of closeness. Conquer the fear of friendship. Tame the fear of love. Allow love to be a part of you and embrace the fears that keep it away.

I pray that we all permit the people in our lives to love us for our beauty, sacredness and uniqueness. Stop the fear. Allow love in.

PONDER THIS: What you love about yourself, you will love in others. What you hate about yourself, you will hate in others. Today, see what you do not like of others and know that this only your mirror.

Open Heart

"Open or Closed Heart – We Decide"

In life you really only have two choices: to live with an open heart or to live with a closed heart: Your choice!

Should you close your heart because of fear, shame, or anger you will not be protecting your heart. You will be missing out on living. You will be living with the fear that the past will come back and that you cannot control the future. You will never be in the Now. Should you open your heart and let go of the fear, shame, or anger you will be letting go of your wounds. You will be choosing a vibrant, full life. Only when your heart is open can love come in.

Love cannot plant its seed and grow in a closed and guarded heart. **DO YOU GET THAT?**

There are no exceptions to this rule. What is not love is an illusion based on the vision of your Shadow. A fallacy fostered by your Shadow to trick you in to complacency.

May you keep your heart wide open for the rest of your life.

PONDER THIS: Where your heart is closed, things cannot thrive. What in your life is not thriving: your work, your relationship with your child, your lover, your parent? See how closed your heart is! For one minute can you open your heart?

The Longest Journey

"Transitioning from Mind to Heart"

What is the longest journey? Is it the drive across Canada? Is it the perilous Silk Road of ancient Eurasia? Is it the spiritual pilgrimage of Camino de Santiego de Compostela across Spain? Maybe it is pursuing education from kindergarten through to PhD? Or possibly studying a martial art from white belt through to black belt? Is life, from birth through to death, the longest journey?

All of these journeys are "long" but none are as long as the road from your mind to your heart. On the spiritual path, the mind can only be the servant of the heart, not the other way around. DO YOU GET THAT?

When you know what your heart wants and when you decide (yes, you get to make that decision) to act on it you will have arrived. You can only get there when your mind is free of the incessant chatter of a legion of fears; fear of intimacy, fear of being inferior, fear of judgement, fear of being alone, fear of making mistakes, and any other fear that may hold sway over you and your ability to embrace life from a place of pure love.

To follow your heart does not mean that you reject your mind. It does not mean that you take what you want because you feel like it. To follow your heart means that your heart and mind are aligned, opened, free of doubts and fears created by the mind.

There are no shortcuts on this road; what does your heart want?

May you dance with your fears on the road from your mind to your heart, comforted by the warm embrace of love. Decide to take the risk and make your heart the guide of your mind. When your heart is your guide and your mind your necessary helper, and only then, will your fears fade away and love radiate out from your entire being.

PONDER THIS: Whether physical, emotional or spiritual, pain comes from your heart and mind not being aligned. Find the pain and find the fears, doubts and negative beliefs that sustain the pain. Are you brave enough to let go of the fears?

Healers and Their Shadow

"Self-Shadow Work for Healers"

The world is full of healers and they can assume many forms. From Reiki masters to past-life regressionists, from massage therapists to quantum touch healers, from psychologists to psychiatrists, from energy workers to sacro-cranial therapists / network chiropractors are all forms of healers and that is but to name a few. It is not wrong to suggest that parents are healers too. So are close friends, sisters and brothers, or anyone else who helps another in a time of need.

Shadow: The concept of "Shadow" is not particularly easy to explain. Inside us all, there is a part of ourselves that we hate and hide. That hidden and hated part is what is called here "the Shadow". Unless we do the alchemical work on the Self, we do not know what we don't know. We hide the Shadow from ourselves so that we are not consciously aware of our disapproval. Without dedicated spiritual investigation, it is unlikely we are aware of the havoc our Shadows create in our day-to-day lives.

Our Shadow is responsible for the drama, the triggers, and the fights that result in the problems within our lives. Our Shadow is a powerful agent of destruction able to create its own reality and sucking us in without us ever being aware we are being manipulated. Projection, judgement, anger, stonewalling, victimization and despair are only a few of the dark manifestations perpetuated by our Shadow. It seeks to keep us scared with confusion, isolating us from the world around us. Our Shadow prevents us from knowing our Light.

Many healers are very knowledgeable in their craft but how many of them are knowledgeable in matter of their Self? How many have journeyed into their Shadow and danced with their Ego? How many have spiritual teachers or guides lighting their path?

I have shared with my students that a therapist, healer or guide should have a teacher of their own. If this healer does not have a teacher for themselves, I feel that this is good cause to turn away. Why? Healing is a form of channeling and the healer is only a vessel or conduit to bring forth what their patient needs. When the healer is tainted by envy, anger, despair, jealousy, injustice and so forth, the tube by which the message is delivered is clogged with gunk. This "gunk" is the emotional baggage of the healer. Healings that are provisioned through dirty conduits hurt people.

Attempting to provide healing without addressing one's Shadow is functionally like filtering one's healing Light through a dirty lens. Unfortunately, in this situation, the Shadow not only hurts the healer but it hurts the patient too.

The Shadow - of a healer, you, or anyone else- is forever present if judgement is still part of your life. How many times a day do you judge people for not being "this" or not being "that"? Even once a day is too much. It means that your Shadow is clouding your Light.

Judgement is always a projection of your own darkness and you need to own up to it. **DO YOU GET THAT?**

If you are part of the healing profession I urge you to find the spiritual teachers and guides you need. Do you have the courage and integrity to do that? You, the healer, are responsible for the life and healing of the people who come to see you. Be honourable, kind, true, and humble in the care of those who trust you. Deal with your Shadow lest it hurt others!

I have students who are healers themselves. By extension I am responsible for the work they do. My students are humble and have the enormous courage required to look at Self and then make the changes that are required. Again and again as life confronts them with new challenges they rise to the occasion and meet their Shadow head-on. Their integrity is awesome and I can vouch for each and every one of them as healers.

If you seek the services of a healer do not hesitate to ask them about their teachers. Ask them about who or what guides them at this moment in time and what these guides are teaching them? If they have finished learning about themselves and have no guides just turn away.

I have spiritual teachers. In turn, my teachers have spiritual teachers of their own. I will have teachers of my own until my last breath. I do mean that.

PONDER THIS: Most people are healers one way or another. Staying by the bedside of your child, your spouse, your parent is a form of healing. Besides wanting to be of service, see if something else is motivating you. Go deep inside yourself and see.

Section II: Water

WATER … THE WORLD OF EMOTIONS

AND FEELINGS.

Light

We each have a Light within us that is unique and
enduring. We are made of this Light. It is our
essence having been named our "Pearl without a
Price" and also called the "Spark of God". Our
purpose and our divinity is found in our Light. The
only thing that prevents us from knowing it better is
our Shadow. Yet, without our Shadow, we could not
know our Light.

If our Light is a pearl then our Shadow is the black
velvet that it is contrasted against allowing its
luminosity to be seen all the clearer. Without the
velvet, the pearl would still shine but it could not shine
as brightly. They are part of a spiritual paradox that
we need to embrace in order to understand ourselves
better.

To know, tame, and befriend our Shadow is to understand the role of the black velvet. Embracing this relationship, we enable ourselves to shine more brightly, pure, and intense aligning ourselves closer to our true Self.

What the Light looks like

"Applying Simple Lessons One at a Time"

This topic is a bit special in that it is a message that was just sent to me by a person on the spiritual path. It is just a letter between a student and a teacher; it is quite simple and yet profound. I thought that it was so inspiring that I could not possibly keep it all to myself. I have changed a few things here and there to preserve this person's anonymity but these changes are very minor. It is about a person who is battling his demons and he is winning!

This is what it looks like to be in the Light. The author has come from a place of total darkness and has worked one day at a time, one step at a time, and has arrived to a place of equanimity and love.

May this letter inspire you as much as it has inspired me.

"Dearest teacher,

I know how many e-mails you get regularly so I will try and keep this as brief as I can but I cannot make any promises.

This past weekend was the weekend of The Bachelor Party – the bachelor party for my friend the Trickster. As you know, this has been a source of anxiety for many reasons. We have discussed these issues and through your guidance, and much reflection about my projections, some of the salt (see first article in book) was rendered innocuous before I went for the event. Still, I approached the event with trepidation. Secretly, I hoped that I would be able to go and enjoy some of the more visceral aspects of a social event like this one, but there was still an undercurrent of fear that pervaded my thoughts.

There was an abundance of salt this past weekend. Each and every time the salt started to sting I found myself quickly, effortlessly, moving to the role of the observer identifying the wound and its cause. Just as quickly as I identified the wound, I reconciled it by loving my Shadow and its fierce dedication to protecting me. I qualified the wound, stanched the infection, loved it until it healed, then proceeded to thank those who unknowingly heaped the salt on me and loved them for their care and commitment to insuring the salt stung. When the dust settled, all the 'triggers' that I was concerned might consume me, were rendered impotent and without the ability to sustain the illusion of a quick fix. Shutting down, stonewalling, withdrawing and isolation, getting angry and starting a fight, picking up a drink and getting drunk – all their intentions and false promises were laid bare and I loved every moment that I was given, the beautiful opportunity to thank these Shadows for what they could teach me.

I have a lifetime to learn what I need to learn from these apparitions but I cannot look on this rocky, unstable road with anything other than love and enthusiasm for I know that I have the power to choose how I embrace my life and the challenges presented therein but more importantly I know that I am good and I have the power to affect good in my environment and the lives of those I am privileged to share this world with.

I know that I am only able to sit here and bask in the afterglow of a weekend full of salt and confrontation with those aspects of myself that have been the source of so much pain because the Universe deigned to send me such a gifted and generous teacher. Thank you.

Much love and gratitude,

Student."

I HOPE YOU GOT THAT!

PONDER THIS: Can you write a letter to the people who are the salt to your wounds simply because they help you know what in you, needs to heal? There is no need to send the letter to anyone. Write it and burn it.

The Monk and the Strawberry

"Appreciating What We Find in the Now"

Here is a little story about being here in the Now. It comes from one of my teachers from many years ago.

Once upon a time a Monk was taking a quiet stroll in the mountains when, all of the sudden, a tiger jumped out in front of him. The monk screamed and started to run in the opposite direction. The Monk ran and ran with the tiger right behind him. The Monk kept running without knowing where he was going. He ran for his life until he came to the edge of the mountain and the ledge overlooking a very deep, very steep cliff face. The Monk was going too fast and could not stop in time; he fell into the void. Grabbing frantically as he fell his hand found purchase on a protruding rock and he hung from this rock with all his strength. Right above the Monk was the tiger. The tiger was baring its teeth in hunger and desperation at being so close to an easy meal. Right below the Monk was a deep, deep fall. The Monk awaited certain death.

Near the rock, a little strawberry was growing. The berry was luscious red and the intoxicating scent of the fruit's perfume hung in the air. It was ripe and ready for eating. The Monk picked the berry and ate it.

As the Monk delighted in eating the berry his heart opened and he said to himself, "Ah, how delicious this strawberry is!". The story ends right here.

The strawberry was delicious – DO YOU GET THAT?

The moment we are born we are on the path towards our deaths. We can walk the path with fear and reluctance, dreading what awaits us (as many of us do) or we can simply enjoy what the Universe has placed in our path in the moment.

Know that fear prevents us from seeing all the wonderful strawberries placed along the path for our journey.

May you all see the strawberries of your days!

PONDER THIS: Today, decide you will enjoy the little things of your day:

- The smell of your soap,

- The taste of your drink,

- The colour of the sky,

- The smile of your colleagues,

- The voice of your loved ones,

…the patience of the universe is waiting for you to wake up.

Burning

"Burning Away Perceptions"

An often forgotten truth to spiritual development is that it is never-ending. Apart from those who believe that enlightenment fosters a sense of indifference, the truth is this path never flows in a straight line and it never ceases to be.

Imagine if you will a three-dimensional spiral drawn out like a stretched spring and traversing along the coils. As time passes, and you work on yourself, you move forward. Your spirituality has focus and it keeps you moving along the same longitude but at times, you will find yourself closer and other times you will find yourself further from that line. You can never be in the same place twice. Things may look the same and even feel the same but the position will constantly change.

Think now of a piano and imagine the chord C sharp. If you play this note further to the left it is lower in the register than if you play it closer to the right of the piano. It is still a C sharp regardless of which end of the keyboard you play it yet, at the same time, it is different. Your progress on your spiritual path is very much the same thing. As you progress you are still "your own note" you but your spiritual resonance is a few octaves higher than it was in the past. Yet you only hear the same chord and not the difference in the octave.

So, you see yourself as "stuck". You will tell me that you are in the same place - the same note, the same dot on the spiral - doomed to repeat the same patterns. Of course you are! Just because you are resonating at a higher frequency your Shadow and your lessons do not change; it is their context that changes! "Higher" does not mean "better". It simply means that you are closer to your own divinity.

Only through the burning of that which is flammable within you (your shame, your anger, your depression, your anger, et cetera) may you discover that which cannot be burned. This is your eternal self, your immutable divinity. **DO YOU GET THAT?**

As you go higher and higher your Shadow becomes more refined. It is more cunning, baffling, and powerful the more real you become. Eventually your triggers will disappear and you will know peace, love, and joy. It is at this moment that your heart is fully open, that your Shadow will be rendered impotent and powerless to deceive you any longer.

May you burn all that is not real within you so that you may see that you are love and love alone.

What is not love is an illusion.

PONDER THIS: Just for one hour, can you focus only on what you like about yourself and others? Can you do that for a whole day?

Shoes

"Replacing Envy with Gratitude"

Once there was a man who complained about his shoes. It started with his shoes being old. Next it was that his shoes hurt his feet. He wanted to replace his shoes but he had no money for a better pair. He began to resent his shoes and he whined, bitched and complained about his "old shoes".

He started to envy those around him who had "better" shoes than he had. The world was unfair and he told everyone that life was hard. With a planet so harsh he began to question what the point of it all was. He no longer had friends and said that he did not need any. He lived alone and wanted no one.

Winter came and he complained that his feet were cold. Spring came and he complained that his shoes got wet in the rain. Summer came and his shoes became too warm. Humbug! Autumn came and all he had left was hate for his shoes.

One day the man with old shoes met a man who had no feet. The man with no feet had no shoes but the man with no feet was happy.

Winter came and the man with no feet remarked that the snow was beautiful. Spring came and the man with no feet reveled in the smell of fresh earth. Summer came and the man with no feet basked in the warmth of the sun. Autumn came and the man with no feet admired the reds in the changing leaves.

The man with no feet lived life with his heart and his heart was open.

The man with no feet smiled at the man who had shoes. The smile was a funnel that channeled his love such that it poured right in to the man who had shoes' heart. The man who had shoes looked down at his old shoes and saw something he never had seen before. He saw that his shoes had faithfully supported him with their love no matter where he wanted them to travel. He opened his heart and realized that his shoes were perfect. More important than that he saw, for the first time, that he had feet!

To focus on what you do not have prevents you from enjoying what you do have. Also, to focus on what you do not have is resistance to the now, and therefore can only bring pain to you and the people around you. DO YOU GET THAT?

I pray that you start loving your shoes and everything else about yourself.

PONDER THIS: For one day, can you focus only on what you do have and banish any thought about what you do not have?

Core

"Differences are as Trivial as Ice Cream"

What flavour of ice cream do you like best? Are you threatened by those who like other flavours of ice cream? Not likely. We all know that someone not sharing our affinity for our favourite flavour of ice cream is not a threat to our person. We may not understand why we prefer the flavours that we do but that is because the mind is not involved – rather we just KNOW that we like the ice cream that we like.

Are you threatened by someone who has a different God than yours? How about those who believe in white supremacy? What if they believe in the reinstatement of the aristocracy condemning many to abject poverty? Conversely what if they believe in limitless abundance?

Understand that we feel our core beliefs are threatened only when we perceive that the conviction and dedication that another holds for their beliefs is lacking in ourselves. When faced with our own faltering convictions we will rely on our mind to justify why we are "right" and others are "wrong".

Only when the mind doubts do we have conflict. When our Core is solid, then we know, there is calm and peace inside. When our beliefs are not steady, we will feel threatened, defend and attack. **DID YOU GET THAT!**

The mind is only useful for logic and analysis. Doubt forever maims it. It is often branded an "imperfect tool" because it can never know.

The heart knows. So does the gut. Our third eye also knows. So does our souls.

Find out what you know. Work on knowing through your experience with and of the Universe. When you know, your Core becomes strong and the fighting stops. The Shadow-hunger of the wanting to be right fades away and you are no longer threatened by the beliefs of others.

PONDER THIS: Instead of being threatened by other people's views, become curious. Stop wanting to be right and show interest. Can you do that with your teenager, your colleague, your mother for one day?

Time

"Providing Ourselves with Space"

When our heart is broken it needs time to heal. Instinctually we may try to staunch the wound swiftly by closing the wound with anger, fear, or addictions (work, alcohol, sex, etc.) but these "quick fixes" will only serve to draw out the healing. It may seem logical to try and close off the pain quickly but it is not respectful to our nature to deny yourself the time to stitch and heal.

Give yourself the time to heal.

When the healing has passed then love, love, and love some more. Keep on loving until your last breath. That is the only thing that we need to do here on earth. Everything else we think is a need is really a "want". Wants are the fuel by which our Shadow is sustained but love is the spark that will start the magic that is our Light.

There is nothing more perfect, connected, special, wise, safe, fun, efficient, power, and important than loving with all our heart. Nothing! **DO YOU GET THAT?**

PONDER THIS: Are you stuck in the past, unable to let go of wrong done unto you or stuck in the good old days where you had it all and no longer have it? If you are stuck in the past, it will become your future.

Sadness

"Welcoming Tears and Sadness"

Sadness can be a disturbing thing. We are not always consciously aware that we are sad. Sometimes the tears manifest themselves in negativity and harsh words. Other times the tears manifest themselves as heavy silences, stonewalling, anger, sulking and, amongst other projections, shutting out those we love. Frequently the mask behind which sadness will lurk is anger.

Our society is afraid of tears and sadness. Tears are a symbol of weakness; sobs and other "soft" emotions are seen as something to hide. Tears are not shameful!

These hidden emotions get passed down through the generations. **DID YOU GET THAT?**

A thousand years of tears have been buried deep in the hearts of our children. They carry our wounds as we carry the wounds of our ancestors. Heal your wounds and spare your children of such a burden!

You may feel a deep sadness from time to time. It can be a reflection of an aching hurt from long ago. Seldom is sadness exclusively the province of current events. As a child you may have been taught that crying was for "sissies" or "babies" so you stopped crying on the outside. A hidden emotion never vanishes, rather it transforms into something rigid and painful unless it is addressed with the utmost respect. What became of your tears?

I pray that tears will cease to bring fear to this world. I pray that the tears shed by your brother and sister will be comforted on your healing shoulder. I pray that crying will break free from the shackles of shame and they never become familiar again.

Tears that are not shed get buried deep within where they fester and rot until they surface, ruining lives all around.

It is okay to be sad. Know that tears, once shed, open a door to freedom, joy and serenity. Cry, but don't bury your eyes for too long as this could be self-indulgence and grandiosity. Lift your head, see the door and discover gratitude.

It is possible to smile through our tears. A smile is like sun through the rain. May you do so and find your rainbow!

PONDER THIS: Could it be that your anger, your sulking, your irritation or your boredom is only sadness disguised in something more socially acceptable?

Section III: Air

AIR ... THE WORLD OF THINKING AND

THE INTELLECT.

The 4 Levels

I believe that there are many levels of consciousness that we can operate on. Through my studies and discussions with my peers, I believe that there are four distinct levels of perception. When I participate in healing work, for myself or others, it is through these levels that I identify where the healing needs to take place. This is because each level is distinct both in form and function.

1st Level: Serpent

The first level of consciousness is called the "Serpent" level. Most people chose to live on this level for their whole lives. It is the most basic level of consciousness and it is rooted in the physical. All problems manifested here are physical in nature and are perceived to result from a specific cause. For example, at the serpent level, a stomach ache would be seen simply as a physical issue requiring a physical remedy, such as herbs or pills. If you live at the serpent level and someone insults you by calling you an "idiot", you will react in kind and insult them in return, say maybe by calling them "stupid". Cause and effect, and eye for an eye - are the only means by which problems are perceived and solved on the Serpent level. Wars are birthed on this level.

2nd Level: Jaguar

The next level above the Serpent level is called the "Jaguar" level. It is the level of the intellect, logic, philosophy, law, medicine, mathematics, and psychology. Those who live on this level cherish the ability to intellectualize. At the jaguar level, more thought and analysis will be put into understanding a stomach ache. The pain may then be rationally associated with emotional patterns that directly precede the ache, such as fighting with loved ones or work related stress. Reconciling the relationships or reducing work stress levels will cure the pain. If you live at the "Jaguar" level and someone decides to insult you, again, by calling you an "idiot", rather than react in kind you may instead reflect on why this person insulted you. You may hypothesize that the other is tired, had a rough childhood, or maybe you will agree that you are in fact being an idiot. What you conclude is irrelevant. What is relevant is that rather than take an eye for an eye, you start trying to understand what is really going on. You start to thirst for the mind.

3rd Level: Hummingbird

The third level is called the "Hummingbird" level. It is where the spiritually advanced aspire to spend their lives. It is the level of symbols, poetry, archetypes, dreams, and energy work. On this level, understanding and knowledge come quickly, without the need to think and rationalize with the mind. At the "Hummingbird" level, a stomach ache may be understood to be the result of fear of being alone in this world. To heal the stomach ache on the "Hummingbird" level, one would have, for example, to heal the fear of loneliness. If you are on this level and someone calls you and "idiot", you would go beyond trying to think why this person is doing that (the "Jaguar" level). You would recognize your Shadow in the person that is insulting you and take ownership and responsibility for your projection. At the "Hummingbird" level, the world is explained in few words, like poetry. A 10 year old child once explained to his mother that God is "the glue that makes hugs stick" (true anecdote). That is the "Hummingbird" level; no more need be said to comprehend the truth in this child's statement. It is at this level that everything has meaning. From the flight of a bird to the ache in your stomach to the bus you missed trying to get to work – it all has potential for growth and gratitude.

4th Level: Eagle

The fourth level is the "Eagle" level. It is the level of the Spirit. No words or concepts exist here, and this is why this level is the most difficult to summarize in words. The "Eagle" level is not a way of thinking or a way to see the world, it is a state. All that exists at this level is a deep and complete understanding fueled by wisdom. It is a state of understanding that can be reached very quickly and suddenly, in only a fraction of a second - an "A-ha!" moment. When you are there, you soar high, like an eagle, and understand the issue in its entirety; you see the stomach ache, the fear of loneliness and you finally know, in every single cell of your body, that the fear is not real. Suddenly, things click, the clouds clear and you see it: "I am not alone in this world" (or whatever lesson you were trying to incorporate). At the "Eagle" level, you just know, you just get it and then an incredible peace washes over you and heals your wounds. Many of my students go to this level to explore the depths of their pain. The Eagle level often leaves my students breathlessly aghast with surprise...surprise and relief. Many often cry from the release it provides. It is rare for anyone to remain on the Eagle level for an extended period of time.

Now that you know the four levels, here is a secret to healing chronic problems: resolution cannot be accomplished on the same level within which it resides. DO YOU GET THAT?

Here is another secret: pain that we allow to shape our lives can only find fertile soil in either the "Serpent" or "Jaguar" levels. When we look at the pain through the lenses of the "Hummingbird" level, we can see through what we once thought was real to discover the truth. It is for this reason that pain, as we know it, cannot take root higher than "Jaguar" – after "Jaguar" there is no more pain, only gratitude and opportunities for growth.

To ascend these levels, all one needs is the knowledge and wisdom to read the language of your inner world. Learning this language is the key. This is what I offer. This is what I teach.

PONDER THIS: Think of any problem you have had for a while. Can you see that problem through the four levels?

Kindness

"Compassion, Understanding Through Kindness"

Kindness is an easy word. To be kind is not complicated. By kindness I do not mean being kind only when people behave the way you want them to behave or turning the other cheek when someone slaps you. Nor do I mean squandering your Light on a rescue mission of someone whom you think needs to be fixed. I mean to choose. Yes, to choose to be in a state of kindness, because this is who you want to be in spite of what is going on around you. It means that your Shadow has calmed down enough for you to see and understand the other person. To be kind is to see the other person as your brother, your sister... someone just like you - yes more like you than you will want to admit at times, who simply needs to be understood. To be kind is to be open. To be kind is a vibration. Be that.

To be kind is a choice, no matter what is going on, on the outside. DO YOU GET THAT?

May your heart see the gratitude in all that surrounds you.

PONDER THIS: No matter how you feel today, can you act and speak with kindness to people around you?

Freedom

"Connecting to Others"

How do you define "freedom"?

Oftentimes I have students tell me that they want freedom. They want to do as they please, travel as they please, come and go as they please and buy what they please. At no point do they talk about the cords and pain that come with this type of freedom. If I were to ask "Why do you need money?" the response I often get is "Money provides freedom and independence." as though this "thing" (e.g., money) can provide all the love, power, control, et cetera that they desire. In this regard, the freedom they covet is the freedom of a child where their Shadow whispers to them that, without this "thing", they will experience no love, have no power, or be unable to control. This is a limited concept of freedom.

To do as you please simply means that you will do as your Shadow dictates: this is not freedom but the most insidious of slavery. In this misconception of freedom you obey the darkest side of yourself. To do as you please means you are the powerless slave to your Shadow.

Spiritual or holy freedom is the sense of exhilaration and openness that we experience when we are aligned with the Universe. In this space as the Universe unfolds so do our horizons to limitless possibilities. **DO YOU GET THAT?**

When we limit ourselves by empowering the whims of the Shadow, we are actually living in a prison. Spiritual freedom is the exact opposite. It is a state of merging and being one with all, while not being enmeshed with the people we share our lives with. We need to be loving yet detached from our children, partners, friends and anyone else so that we can be alone, a thread within the fabric of the Universe. When we give ourselves to friends, family, money, travel, et cetera we put our Shadow first and foremost in our lives. We refuse Oneness and guarantee the pain that is to come. Giving away our love, power, and control to another person, situation, or thing is a recipe for drama that will leave us spinning in the middle of the night!

How do we remain in the paradox centered and separate while being one with all? The trick is to keep our own Core while we exercise our ability to align ourselves with the unfolding of the Universe. This is the freedom that comes from our will meeting the will of the Universe. This is the freedom of being embraced lovingly by it as all unfolds exactly as it should. Our Shadows will try and tell us the Universe is an unloving terror and encourage us to sacrifice our Core. It will whisper to us to merge and enmesh with others, to be co-dependent, to abuse alcohol and drugs, to exploit sex, as well as a variety of other distractions and simple gratifications but, with time, the hollowness of these diversions will overcome us. This is slavery, not freedom.

It takes a lifetime to forgo our Shadow and embrace our Light so that we can live with such limitless freedom that we know we can reach out and touch the stars. Fortunately a lifetime is exactly what you have and there is one simple step.

To be free is to be lovingly One with the Now.

PONDER THIS: Where you feel the most stuck offers the greatest potential for freedom. How do you contribute to your prison?

Love is Like Rain

"Unconditional Love"

Love is like rain. It falls on everyone regardless of what you have done, said, or thought. Saints and sinners alike are wrapped within its embrace without judgement or reserve.

When you close your heart because others do not behave like you want them to behave, then love cannot come in. Love does not know anything about control, manipulation, or revenge because love comes without conditions. It does not matter if the people in question are part of your life, people you are familiar with, or people in the media – withholding love is like denying rain to withered crops.

The Universe draws no distinction on how or to whom it showers love. It rains its love down on everyone. **DO YOU GET THAT?**

May you be like the rain and shower the love that you are on the whole world. Try it – you may find it easier than you thought.

PONDER THIS: Today, just for one minute, can you find love for one person who has not behaved the way you wanted them to behave? Can you do this for two minutes?

To Love

"Just Love – Not a Choice"

To love with one's whole heart is not a choice – it is a shared aspiration and your destiny as a human being. The path of an open heart is a journey that we all share. Paths are, of course, roads and the "spiritual" road is about getting closer to Spirit. Getting closer to "Spirit" (God, Dao, the Creator, Allah, et cetera) requires that you relax your heart and welcome love. No excuses. No Shadow-driven babble.

Just love. **DO YOU GET THAT?**

It is that simple.

PONDER THIS: For one minute, can you just have love in your heart? Just one minute …

Be Present Be still

"Stillness to Observe"

Be still! Just for a moment, be still and look – be still and be present.

Most, if not all, of us fight stillness. In the stillness you exist naked and exposed. The Presence of Self is there; this is your Essence, it is the Pearl without a Price. This can be intimidating such that the fear drives us to run away from our own divinity.

How do we run? Let me count the ways.

Some run by pushing the world away from them with negativity. Some run by wearing rose coloured glasses forever pretending that all is fine and good. Some run by stonewalling and sulking. Some run by finding fault in others while never acknowledging the fault in themselves. Blaming, yelling, lying, denying, or fighting are the sprints at the start of a marathon. Self-medicating through the abuse of alcohol, drugs, work, gambling, shopping, food, or sex are other means of running. Some prefer to run by spending hours in front of the television or video games. Some run by creating artificial drama. Some can even run by going to ashrams to meditate away the pain.

Stop the running. Stop and see yourself and the miraculous world you live in. Above all else admit that you are running!

Stop running and step into the stillness. If you are still, what will you see?

You may see that your anger at your lover is really a depression you have been burdened with since childhood. You may see that your frustration at your boss is really a reflection of your father who was never there for you. You may see that you have tears that need to be shed. You may see that loneliness has always been a part of you and not the result of a recent event such as your children leaving home. You may see that you have tried to control the whole world around you attempting to bend it to your will and by making it "perfect". You may see that your arrogance is really your own shame of being different and trying to fit in. You may see that you have used others to fulfill your own ambitions. You may see that no amount of knowledge will make the world safer for you than it is right now. You may see that self-value can never be found in the opinions of others. You may see that the image you are projecting onto the world is a complete lie. You may see that all your judgements are the reflection of your own Shadow and that you are the one responsible for the drama in your life.

Be still and see the truth; that you can choose to open your heart -way wide and wider still- and know that you are a child of the Universe and you are perfect as you are now in this moment.

Once upon a time there was a man who turned around and saw he had a Shadow. He made one step forward and saw that his Shadow was still with him. He did not like his Shadow and started to run in an attempt to get rid of it. He looked back and saw that his Shadow followed him, so he ran faster. The Shadow was still there and so determined, he ran faster and faster, to no avail, because his Shadow never left him. He ran for years and years traversing the Earth ten times, yet his Shadow was always there. He ran his whole life when all he had to do was stop running and sit under a tree.

All you have to do is be still. There is nowhere to run. **DO YOU GET THAT?**

I pray that you find your tree and sit. I pray that you find the stillness that will set you free. I pray that you may reflect on yourself, eventually coming to know your divinity. I pray that you see that there is only love. I pray that you see that what you may perceive as not being "love" is just an illusion.

PONDER THIS: Before you start running stop and be still for one minute! Connect with whatever is inside. Can you be still for two minutes? Five minutes?

What We See

"Know Ourselves, Know God"

Many of my students would like to understand God and the Universe. To that objective I say; "Give it up! Have the humility to admit that god and the universe(s) (yes, there is probably more than one) cannot be grasped by your mind. Your intellect is too small to think like 'God'."

Concepts such as divine justice and divine perfection are difficult to incorporate in to one's life. The analytical ego, doubtful mind will forever judge an event as "fair" or "unfair", "perfect" or "imperfect", "good" or "bad" depending on the perception of the individual. This reality has little to do with the reality of God.

We do not see things as they are but as we are. **Do YOU GET THAT?**

Know that we see with what is behind our eyes and seldom do we actually see what is in front of our eyes.

We cannot understand God (or whatever you wish to call it) but we can come to know God. Faith is not a prerequisite to knowing. Faith is for those who doubt.

To know yourself is to understand the reality that you create. To know your fears is to see how you see the world.

PONDER THIS: Listen carefully to people's perspective about a movie, a meeting, a news broadcast. Broaden your horizon and your vision by staying away from right and wrong. Can you do this for one week?

Be What it is That You Want

"Live That Which You Want Most"

What do you want?

Do you want love? Maybe you want respect? What about abundance? Do you want (real) friendships? Do you want knowledge? Maybe you want serenity, "letting go", and peace? Do you want sobriety and recovery?

To get what you want you need only do one thing – be what it is that you want. At every opportunity you give that which you want, and as what you emit is what you attract, you will attract what you want from your deepest self.

We can only give what we do not have and receive what we already have. So give that which you do not have and you will create miracles. **Do you get that?**

Fill yourself full by giving. When you are giving, be mindful to do so without thought of receiving anything in return. If you can do that you will be truly giving and not investing.

Give that which you do not have and you will be what you want most.

PONDER THIS: For one day, or perhaps one week, decide to give respect (or love, or listening, etc.) to everyone. The people with whom it is hardest are often the people from whom you demand (beg?) respect. Give them more. Note what happens.

Section IV: Earth

EARTH … THE WORLD OF MANIFESTATION,

THE TANGIBLE AND CONCRETE WORLD

Wisdom

Many people confuse information and wisdom. The truth is that they are polar opposites. One can have lots of information but no wisdom. Information is the knowing how to do something but wisdom is the act of living the task.

Learning something, anything, needs to be done in stages. The spiritual path is no different from learning; it must be done in stages. The spiritual path can be represented in four levels. These four levels are reflected in Tarot suits, shamanic teachings, The 4 Levels (as described at the beginning of Section III) and many other areas.

1st Stage: Information

Information is the antidote to ignorance but you need to be able to absorb the information you are collecting.

The way you absorb information depends on many factors but it is accentuated by your knowledge and familiarity with yourself.

When I teach and first provide information I offer it using as many ways as I can to address the needs of my students. Some students are visual, while others are auditory, but others may be kinesthetic. Some are detailed oriented and others are turned off by details. You need to become more familiar with what type of a student you are so you can best maximize your absorption of the information you collect.

How do you think that you best understand and retain information?

2nd Stage: Understanding

You need to understand what you learn. Not just say *"Ya, ya, I get it"* and assume that you not only comprehend the words as they are spoken but what they also represent.

3rd Stage: Comprehension

You need to know how to apply what you have understood; to integrate it in to your understanding and perception of the world around you. This is integration and incorporation of knowledge.

4th Stage: Wisdom

You need to actually be able to act on what you have learned; you need to be able to act at the right moment and without effort. When you resist acting on knowledge (with words, with body, with thoughts) your Shadow takes over. When you act on knowledge you move into the Light. To be wise is to be real and present.

Wisdom is actually the will to bring into your day to day life the knowledge you have. DO YOU GET THAT?

Knowledge without action is absurd. It is trying to learn how to swim from a book but never getting in to the water. Until you get in to the water and actually swim you have accomplished little. Some of my students resist getting in to the water; they resist the "doing". They collect the information but never accomplish the homework. They resist wisdom!

For all your questions, all your pain, and all your dramas I say this: The answer is very, very close to you and it will reveal itself to you only when you are willing to change your thoughts, your actions, and open your heart. The decision is yours whether to allow this to happen or not. You get to decide.

Get wise – now go out and "act wise"!

PONDER THIS: Make an inventory of areas in your life where you have knowledge and little wisdom. Here are a few examples:

- Yeah, I know I shouldn't take it personally but I can't help it!

- Yeah, I know I should take care of my body but it's too hard!

- Yeah, I know I should not yell at the kids but they trigger me so much!

- Yeah, I know I should not sulk and shut down but I am so hurt!

Find the fear that is the blockage to wisdom, change and be free!

Surrendering

"Surrender to Failure, Embracing Wisdom"

The following applies only to those of you who are interested in the Path of Surrender.

I often hear my students say that they want to surrender or that they have surrendered to the will of the Universe. Yet, I wonder why they are still sad, angry or ashamed. The answer is not complicated; they have confused "yielding" with "surrender". Yielding causes pain and leaves us feeling like we have lost and the Universe has won. Whereas surrendering brings peace of mind and love to the heart and power to the belly.

In order to truly surrender, you need to say "I have failed at this! I have failed and now I surrender to the will of the Universe!" "This" could be money, addiction, anger, health, love, or something else you cherish; it does not matter. What matters is that you have truly surrendered; it must pulse outwards from your bones, your marrow, from the very end of your Shadow so that you might accept and acknowledge that you have failed. Without acknowledgement of failure there can be no surrender - only yielding. Until you accept failure, your Shadow will come back and try to control the situation in one way or another. You will know that your "surrender" is fake because there will be no peace.

To surrender is to align your will to the will of the Universe. Nothing will give you more peace, love, authenticity, Oneness, safety, Light, power than surrender. **DO YOU GET THAT?**

What you do not surrender will dominate your dreams. It will dominate your conversations with others. You will study books and other sources of knowledge about it. Your head will tell you that this should not be so and that the Universe is not perfect. Despite all this, your heart will yearn for something that is not part of your reality. Your surrender will still be false.

To fully understand surrendering, know that failing means there is nothing else you can DO. Absolutely nothing.

The humility of failing will guide you to freedom from the pain.

So, if your goal is to surrender then you need to carry on until you can say you have tried everything, and that you are powerless in the face of this problem. Do this so that you may accept your failure and embrace surrendering to a higher authority. Then and only then will you feel relief. Allow the waves of relief to crest over you, and while you are taken by its flow, you will find perfection in everything. When you see that everything is perfect the way it is, right now and always, then you have surrendered.

First say, "I have failed." Then say, "I surrender to the wisdom of the Universe."

Once you believe wholly in those two statements you will find the precious serenity and lightness of being that awaits you.

I pray for peace to enter your heart.

PONDER THIS: Where your thoughts are most of the day is where you have not surrendered. Be aware of your fight. If there is nothing you can do about the situation, surrender and let it go.

Love (It is a Choice!)

"Surrendering to Allow Love to Flow"

It is through love that we can embrace our most authentic state. To live with a heart infused with love is the one great truth to which one should aspire.

A heart flowing with love becomes like a river; the more open our hearts are, the more powerful the current. The river of wealth that awaits us is directly proportional to the alignment of our soul with our true nature.

When we fear surrender we close our heart. We shut down, believing that we will be spared undue pain. Instead we are greeted with a cruel truth; that the more closed our heart is, the less alignment we experience and the more choked our rivers become. Eventually, if we allow ourselves to become too closed, wealth is no longer part of our lives and our energy gets stuck. Abundance, in all its forms (e.g., money, health, love, happiness, et cetera), will cease to flow.

Surrender is for the brave for they do not allow fear to lead the way. DO YOU GET THAT?

To surrender is to relinquish all forms of control. It is not unlike riding a bicycle where, once we are proficient enough, we can adeptly manage what we may encounter. When we encounter the pedestrian walking on the side of the road, the car parked in the lane – none of these obstacles will present us with a challenge. We do not worry about the obstacles appearing and we do not try to exert control. We just pedal and do what we need to, when we need to do it. This is the essence of surrender and it is the foundation for love.

Take a moment right now and close your eyes. With your eyes shut try to love every facet of your life. Your ex-partner, the pain in your back, the lilac blooms in front of your house, a child with a balloon, the smile of a stranger on the bus, the bill sitting on your desk waiting to be paid....love all of it with your heart and soul. Let your heart expand to embrace every aspect of your life and just be...just for a moment.

When aligned with your true nature, regardless of what it may be, your path will flow easily throughout the rest of your life. Every moment will be awe-inspiring allowing you to live with love in a perfect river of cherished moments. Your Shadow will cease its judgement of good and bad; everything will just be as it is and you will love it for the perfection that it is. Then, and only then, will love consume your every moment.

Why would you want anything else?

PONDER THIS: For one hour, let go of labelling people, events, circumstances, and physical conditions as "good" or "bad". Life just is. Pain just is. Can you find gratitude for everything for one hour (without cynicism)? Can you do this for one day?

Love: the Most Powerful Energy

"Unconditional Loving Energy"

Sometimes, it is hard to love. Someone may lie to you, lead you astray, be wantonly mean towards you, invade your personal space, or just behave hurtfully and you withdraw into yourself, or lash out, unwilling to love in return. In these moments, it is important to see the Light shining from within for each and every person around you. You need to embrace that Light and just love them for whom they are. This is not about sending love but about being Love.

Love is the most powerful energy around. It is more powerful than any pain or hurt another person's Shadow can inflict on you.

Be love. It does not mean that you agree, condone, live with, or befriend. It means that you choose to radiate (not send) love no matter what is going on. Do YOU GET THAT?

PONDER THIS: As difficult as it is to accept, what you do not like about others is only a projection of what you do not like about yourself.

Spiritual Intelligence

"A Measure of the Strength of the Core"

There are many types of intelligence. The most commonly measured is intellectual intelligence which is often equated with IQ tests. This is but one small part of the "intelligence" that is the sum of an individual. Emotional intelligence has been gaining popularity and becoming more mainstream. Functionally it is broken down in to two parts; the external emotional understanding of others (how good we are at knowing how others feel) and the internal emotional understanding of one's self (how well do we know our own feelings). Yet, there are other types of intelligence in this world.

There is spatial intelligence which helps when we are trying to pile things neatly in the trunk of a car. There is temporal intelligence which gives us the ability to know what time (in the linear sense of the word) it is without wearing a watch. There is navigational intelligence which gives us the ability to sense which way is North at all times. There is mathematical intelligence, musical intelligence and so on and so on. One type of intelligence that stands out from all the others is spiritual intelligence.

Unlike the other types of "intelligence," spiritual intelligence is hard to quantify. It is fluid, making it difficult to measure. It is the ability and willingness to comfortably hold your Core as you hold inside yourself one or more conflicting ideas without losing your Core. The greater the ability to remain centered in the face of such contradictions, the greater your spiritual intelligence. You do not have to agree, condone, or even embrace these ideas but you do have to remain centered, unmoved and unaffected (un-triggered) and curious, by someone who has a contradictory conviction to yourself.

The vegetarian who is comfortable with eating meat under specific circumstances that dictate that meat is eaten is a good example. The present Dalai Lama, a vegetarian, will eat meat when it is served to him by others without losing his center and getting triggered by such a contradiction to his own beliefs. He knows, in his Core, that he is a vegetarian and that eating meat does not lessen the strength of his Core. If the choice was instead to get annoyed or angry with friends/hosts (i.e. that they should "know better"), or indulge in any other judgement and/or protest then the quotient for retaining one's Core goes down and spiritual intelligence is not met.

Spiritual intelligence is a question of the strength of your Core; DO YOU GET THAT?

When we are triggered by the opinions of others we need to work on our Core. We must hunt the projection within and rise above it to the point where we are One with All. From this altitude there is no one to fight, we have no enemies on the outside. We remain serene no matter what is going on outside.

PONDER THIS: For one week can you show curiosity for the opinion of others especially when you do not agree. Can you stop feeling attacked and simply listen?

Miracles

"The Magic of Alchemy and Manifestation"

We all want miracles in our lives. Through these miracles we hope and pray that they will make us proud or happy or strong or allow us to achieve "perfection". Miracles happen every day. The secret to manifesting a miracle is to do something outside of your comfort zone. These things, the things that take you outside the space where you are safe, need be done consistently and frequently.

- Do you want to become a concert pianist? The miracle of becoming a concert pianist will only happen if you practice piano over and over again.

- Do you want to be accepted? The miracle of acceptance will only come after you have battled shame over and over again.

- Do you want to have faith? The miracle of faith will only happen when you have faced your fears over and over again.

- Do you want to find peace and serenity? The miracle of peace and serenity will only happen if you battle against control over and over again.

We all can accomplish miracles if we put our mind, body, and soul in to it. We need to commit ourselves to taking ourselves beyond what we consider safe or easy.

The Universe is waiting to give us all that we desire but it longs for the clarity of the complete commitment that comes from living outside our comfort zones consistently and frequently. Leveraging this clarity, we signal loud and clear what miracles we want to manifest. No one else can do it for you. DO YOU GET THAT?

The magic of manifestation and the alchemy that transforms us comes from focus, work, and going the extra one percent every day as often and regularly as we can. This is the way of the Magician, the Warrior of Light, and the Miracle Worker.

PONDER THIS: For one month and every day of that month do one thing outside your comfort zone:

- Expressing your feelings with kindness and truth;

- Refusing procrastination;

- Banishing nagging at family members;

- Really listening without giving advice;

- Sharing time and other resources.

Can you see little miracles happening around you?

The "Other" Reality

"Listening For God in Our Silence"

We all believe that we see reality the way it is meant to be seen. We never could imagine ("imagine" is the correct word) that the reality we see is a fantasy and a projection of our creation. Human beings see the world the way they are and not the way the world is. We tend to see what is behind our eyes and not what is in front of our eyes.

What is the true reality? What does it look like? Can there be another reality?

Finding the "other reality" is even harder than seeing what it is. This other reality is the language of "God"; it is the inner language of our souls. We all have the ability to converse in this language. This language is the essence of who we are and it is the only part of us that understands divinity. Divinity can be God, Allah, magic, the Dao, miracles, The Great Spirit, or the collective unconscious but one thing is certain – we can never understand it with logic. Logic hinders our ability to converse in the inner language of our souls.

Know that it is our purpose to find and understand our divine dialect then share it with all human beings. This is what some people would call their "higher purpose". This "purpose" (and everyone has one – the Universe never creates anything for no purpose) is finding our essence and sharing it. It is as simple as that.

"How do I find this secret language so that I might discern my purpose to share with all humanity?"

This is a question we all must entertain. To find our path we need to be quiet inside of ourselves. We need to know (and love) our Shadows or else the path will remain hidden. It takes time. It takes work. It takes determination, humility, awe, and knowledge.

Sssshh! Are you quiet inside? Can you hear your soul speaking to you? The "other reality" is wrapped in that silence and once you can hear your soul you will find it. **DO YOU GET THAT?**

Living your higher purpose is the other reality that illuminates your path with an intense Light that shines on your every step along the way.

PONDER THIS: Write a few lines describing what this planet is like: dangerous, mysterious, miraculous, loving, mean etc. What does it say about you? We see with what is behind of our eyes. So be the change you want to see.

Contact Information

Bernadette Kaye welcomes inquiries with respect to her work. You may contact her at the following email: didyougetthat@yahoo.com

Please note, emails from Bernadette are minimal! Emails are sent out when:

- a newsletter is released,

- her courses are announced once a year, and

- an in depth description is provided, before each course.

Amanda Jensen, is the artist who created the insightful design for the cover page of this book! She welcomes inquiries regarding her work. You may order prints of the cover page from this book directly from Amanda.

Her email amandacjensen@live.ca and

Website: www.acjensen.ca

Notes

Lightning Source UK Ltd.
Milton Keynes UK
UKHW041822091218
333730UK00001B/111/P